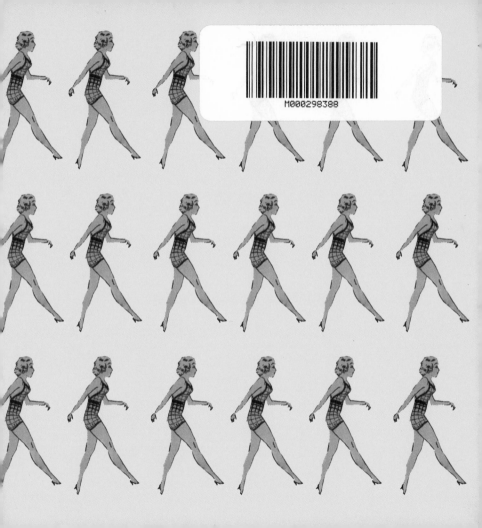

real wisdom
from
unreal women

real wisdom
from
unreal women

risa palazzo

CICO BOOKS
LONDON NEW YORK

ART SAYS IN PICTURES WHAT CANNOT BE SAID IN WORDS

This book is dedicated to my family.

Published in 2013 by CICO Books
An imprint of Ryland Peters & Small Ltd
20–21 Jockey's Fields,   519 Broadway, 5th Floor,
London WC1R 4BW   New York, NY 10012

www.cicobooks.com

10 9 8 7 6 5 4 3 2 1

ISBN: 978 1 908862 75 4

Printed in China

Artworks and text: Risa Palazzo
Editor: Penny Craig
Designer: Mark Latter

For digital editions, visit www.cicobooks.com/apps.php

contents

*give
more
than
you
receive*

Introduction

One of the most beautiful and fascinating women in the world is made not of flesh but of paint. She draws visitors from every continent, who ponder the source of her beguiling smile. Leonardo da Vinci's Mona Lisa is not a real woman. She is forever settled in the same pose, hands gently crossed, silent and intoxicating as a rose, and yet she crosses the line between the concrete and the intangible. So it is with the unreal women in this book. Some, like da Vinci's masterpiece are two-dimensional figures captured on canvas. Others are made of paper, plastic, wood, or stone. Although mute, each manages to convey a message that deserves to be heard. The images are of paintings I have done or purchased, while all of the dolls, figurines, family photographs, and assorted objects are from my own collection. I chose faces I felt most clearly expressed emotions, using color and collage techniques for the greatest effect. You will no doubt notice that I believe perfection is highly over-rated. It is the assorted dings, dents, and cracks that tell the best stories.

The line between the real and the unreal has intrigued me since I was a child. My first doll, a little rubber girl with blinking blue eyes and tiny white plastic teeth was as real to me as a baby sister. I was captivated by the movies "One Touch of Venus" and "Mr. Peabody and the Mermaid" because they starred women who were real but unreal at the same time: one was a statue who alternated between flesh and marble, while the other was half woman and half fish! In "The After Hours," my favorite episode of Rod Serling's TV series "The Twilight Zone," department store mannequins come to life the moment the store closes for the night.

It is my hope that you relinquish your belief in what is real and what isn't and listen to what the women populating this little book have waited so long to tell you.

Risa Palazzo

Eyes up,
feet on the ground.

life

SEARCH THE WORLD

AND THE SEVEN SEAS.

CHANCES ARE WHAT YOU WANT

YOU ALREADY HAVE.

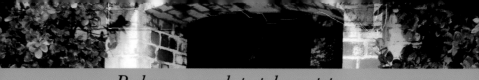

*Be brave enough to take a step
into a different world*

reach
for
what
you
think is
unreachable

You can't win the race every time.

The journey matters more than the finish-line.

YOU ARE
A QUEEN
TO SOMEONE

Buy a card, pick up a pen.

Write a heartfelt message.

No birthday emails.

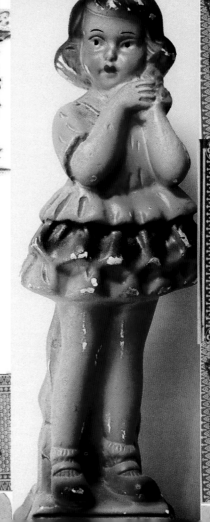

THE SALTY AIR,
THE PIER,
THE GIGGLING CHILDREN.
REMEMBER THAT
LIFE IS BEAUTIFUL.

Dented the car.

Lost the wallet.

Spilled ink on the new rug.

Old age is an honor not a curse.

Red lipstick

is a perfect

cure-all.

APPRECIATE THE TENDER CREATURES
IN YOUR OWN BACKYARD

**your
weight
is a
number**

**not a
definition
of who
you are**

NOTICE OUR SIMILARITIES
NOT OUR DIFFERENCES AND SHAKE HANDS.

DANCING IS SO MUCH

MORE FUN

THAN THE TREADMILL

AND BURNS

JUST AS MANY CALORIES

NOBODY CARES
IF IT'S STORE-BOUGHT

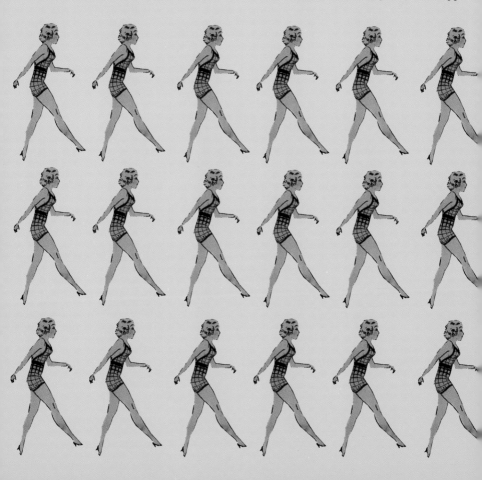

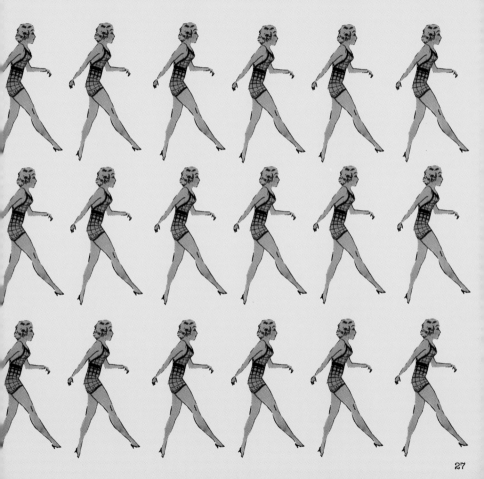

Love

Bring a little
color into
someone's
black and
white world

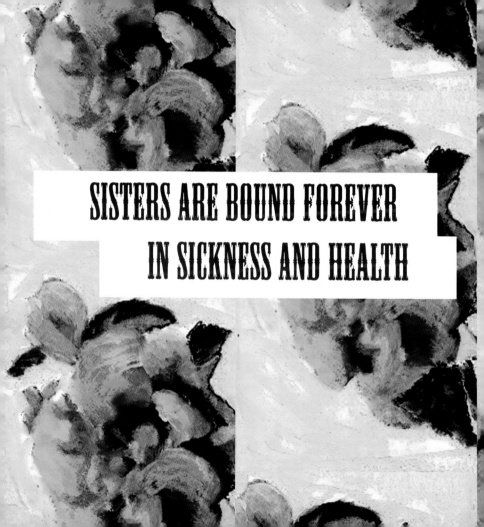

SISTERS ARE BOUND FOREVER
IN SICKNESS AND HEALTH

A LITTLE
HEALTHY
COMPETITION

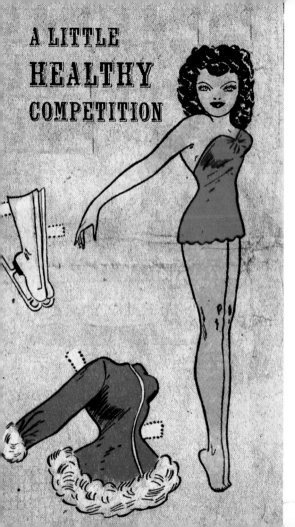

KEEPS A
GIRL
ON HER
TOES

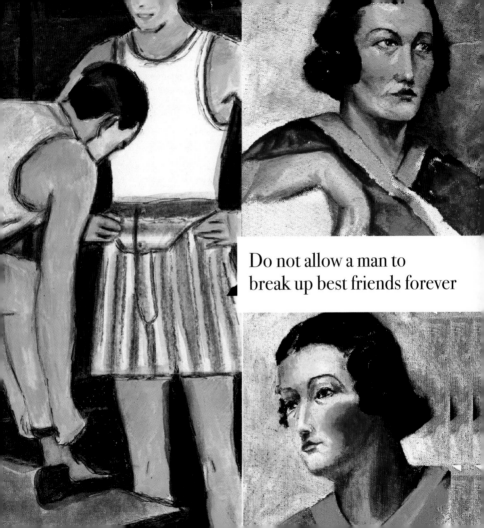

Do not allow a man to break up best friends forever

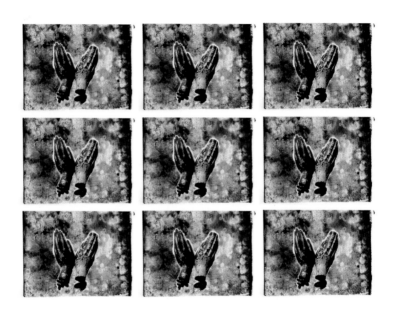

A soft touch.

An encouraging pat. A playful tickle.

Our hands are magical instruments of love.

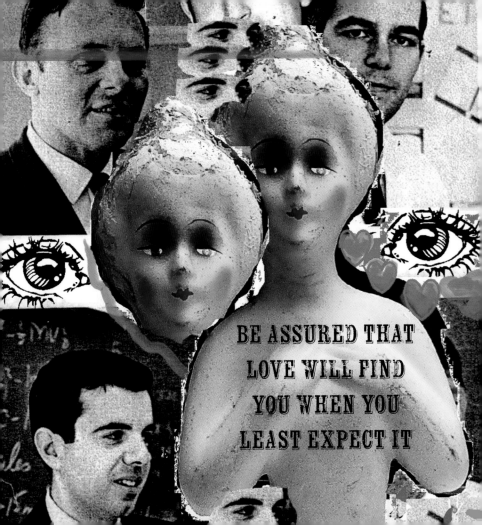

BE ASSURED THAT
LOVE WILL FIND
YOU WHEN YOU
LEAST EXPECT IT

It's still free
to dream

THE

bloom

MAY BE OFF THE

rose

BUT YOU
ARE FOREVER

lovely

CALL YOUR MOTHER

YOU'LL MISS
THOSE CALLS
WHEN SHE IS GONE

express your emotions, without

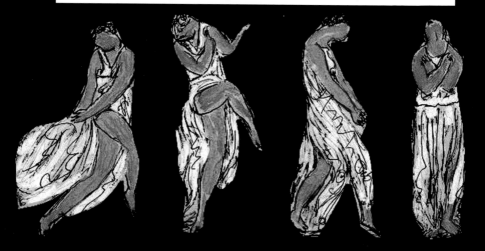

allowing them to control you

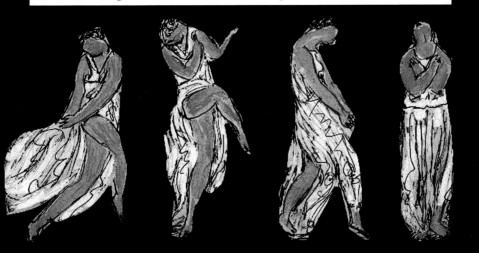

Men have sculpted us
for centuries
because we
are beautiful,
fascinating
creatures

When
  you
    fall
       to
         pieces

know you are
strong enough
to pull yourself
together again.

SORROWS

Nobody ever promised life would be easy. But your hard work will be rewarded.

BLING WILL
NOT MEND
A BROKEN
HEART.

BUT IT HELPS.

Remember the ancestors who paved your way in a new land

keep away
from the
bad boys

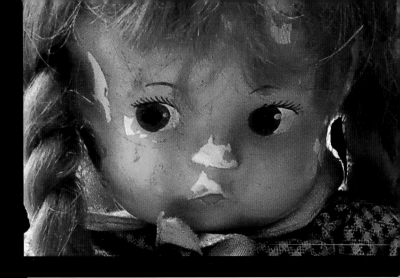

If he hit you once, he'll hit you again.

Believe it. And leave.

EVEN A FAITHFUL
HUSBAND MAY BE
TEMPTED TO STRAY.

BEWARE
THE AU PAIR.

OLD WOUNDS
SOMETIMES
NEVER HEAL.

ACCEPT THEM
AND MOVE ON.

seeing *the*
world

through

rose-tinted
glasses

works
for me

Angels may or may not exist.

But belief in them helps smooth a rough road.

Offer shelter to those in need

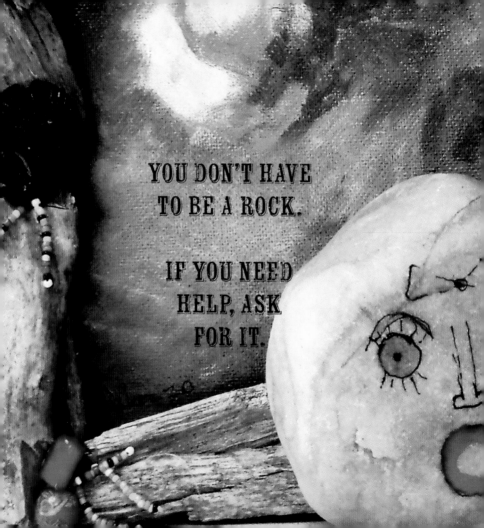

Looking down on others signals

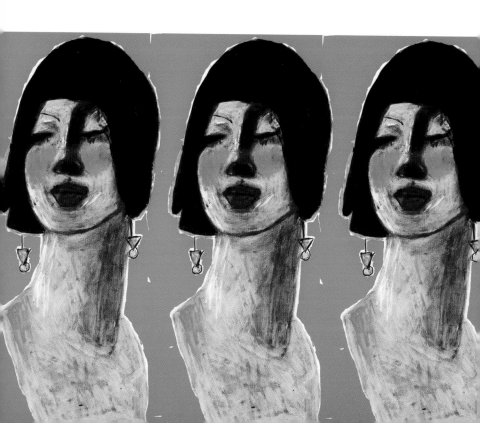

a need for greater self-esteem

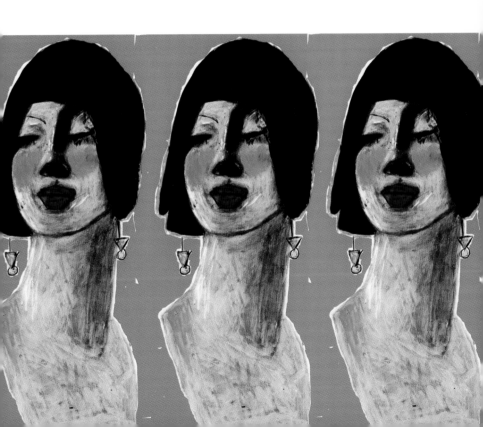

Dear ones we have lost
come to life in our memories

Acknowledgments

I wish to thank my husband, Albert, for his unflagging
support and encouragement always; our son David for assisting
with the photography; and our son, Andrew, for helping his
technologically-challenged mother. A big thank you to Cindy
Richards for taking on this project, to editors Clare Sayer and
Penny Craig, and to art director Sally Powell and the talented
designers at Cico Books. Additionally, I must thank the wonderfully
gracious artist/designer, Gloria Vanderbilt, whose kind personal
letters have been such sources of joy to me through the years,
and whose remarkable collages and sense of spirit have had
such a strong impact on my work and life.

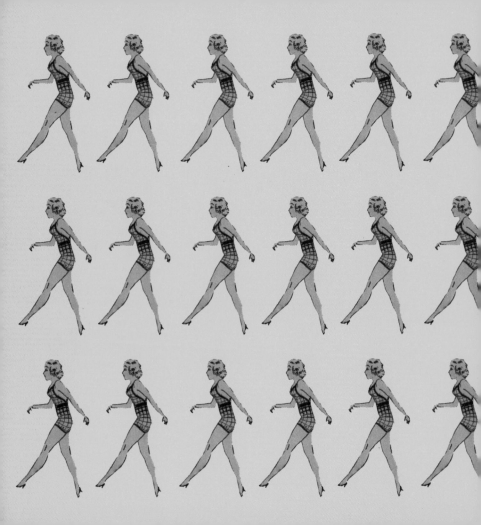